Fear factor

YUCK!

GROSSEST STUNTS EVER!

By Jesse Leon McCann

SCHOLASTIC INC.

New York   Toronto   London   Auckland   Sydney

Mexico City   New Delhi   Hong Kong   Buenos Aires

For my daughter Amanda, fearless as a child,
now a brave young woman

The stunts from *Fear Factor* described in this book were designed and supervised by trained professionals. They are extremely dangerous and should not be attempted by anyone, anywhere, anytime.

Photo Credits: Alamy A4NEE2 rat © Eureka/Alamy; Alamy RF AC523F grasshopper © Ingram Publishing/Alamy; Picture Quest (RF) 22483081 broken glass © James Dawson/Image Farm/PictureQuest; SODA OS18077 rat © Photodisc via SODA

ISBN 0-439-79050-6

Fear Factor ™ & © 2005 Endemol Netherlands B.V.

Published by Scholastic Inc.
SCHOLASTIC and associated logos are trademarks and/or registered trademarks of Scholastic Inc.

12 11 10 9 8 7 6 5 4 3 2 1   5 6 7 8 9/0

Designed by Michelle Martinez Design, Inc.
Printed in the U.S.A.
First printing, September 2005

Introduction

The Gross Factor

Since its premiere five years ago, *Fear Factor* has become a phenomenon seen all over the world.

While the dangerous stunts are very popular, most people's favorite part of each episode is the gross part. You know, the part where somebody has to crawl into a pool filled with buffalo guts, or eat a giraffe's esophagus, or let a thousand screaming cockroaches crawl over them? This book will focus on those parts . . . the gross parts . . . the gag-and-giggle, squeal-and-scream "I can't believe they just did that" gross parts. We'll describe some of the most revolting stunts in detail, and even rate them with our *Fear Factor* Yuck-O-Meter—one star ★ being a little gross, five stars ★★★★★ being gut-wrenchingly gross.

But there's a whole lot more in this book! Interviews with contestants from the show, nauseating puzzles, fearsome stunt records, terrifyingly gross trivia and quizzes, and pictures you won't want to look at while eating! We'll also talk about different phobias. Phobias are persistent fears that sometimes freak people out. We'll list some of the more interesting phobias—like phobophobia, which is the fear of phobias.

So, on with the show!

But before we do—this important warning:

The stunts from *Fear Factor* described in this book were designed and supervised by trained professionals. They are *extremely dangerous* and should **not be attempted** . . . by anyone . . . anywhere . . . anytime!

REPULSIVE RECORDS!

STATS FOR SOME SERIOUSLY GROSS *FEAR FACTOR* STUNTS

- Record for the fastest team to trudge through a long, deep trench filled with cow parts (guts, liver, heart, brains, etc.), gnawing the flesh from cow jawbones, filling a glass with the flesh, grinding the flesh, and swallowing it all: 13 minutes, 8 seconds.

  ### YUCK-O-METER RATING ★★★

- Quickest time for a player to transfer a blended maggot mixture with his mouth into a shake glass filled with live flies, and, once the glass was full, drink the entire contents of the glass: 2 minutes, 19.4 seconds.

  ### YUCK-O-METER RATING ★★★★★

- Record weight for players scooping up a mixture of super worms, red worms, stink beetles, grasshoppers, and crickets all smashed onto a car windshield using only their mouths, and transferring the squashed bugs to a scale in two minutes: 7 3/8 ounces.

  ### YUCK-O-METER RATING ★★★★★

- Fastest time eating 12 live snails: 44.1 seconds.

  ### YUCK-O-METER RATING ★★★★★

- The most worm, cricker, scorpion, and millipede mush made by one sibling and eaten by the other in three minutes: 1 pound, 13.85 ounces.

  ### YUCK-O-METER RATING ★★★★

- Best time for bobbing for large chunks of cheese in a fondue pot filled with a melted mess of the moldiest, stinkiest cheeses around and then eating five live giant horse grasshoppers: 1 minute, 44.5 seconds.

  ### YUCK-O-METER RATING ★★★★

TASTES FROM OTHER NATIONS . . . THAT YOU MAY FIND DISTASTEFUL!

- In China, don't be surprised if they serve you a dish of mustard sauce over duck feet!

- When in France, if you order escargot, you'll be eating snails!

- If you travel through Turkey, you may walk into a restaurant lined with precooked sheep's heads ready to eat!

- Speaking of sheep, when in Scotland, haggis will be on most menus. This delicacy is various animal organs boiled inside a sheep's stomach!

- Iceland has a treat called rotted shark. It's a shark that's been buried underground and left to ferment for many years—served and eaten frozen so the stinky smell doesn't fill up the restaurant!

- A delicacy in Thailand is bird's nest soup. Cooks take a swallow's nest and boil it with some veggies and herbs. Swallow saliva, which is used to hold the twigs together, is supposed to be very tasty and nutritious!

APPALLING PUZZLER!

FILL IN THE BLANKS AND SOLVE STOMACH-TURNING *FEAR FACTOR* CROSSWORD #1:

ACROSS

5. Fill in the blank: Madagascar hissing _____. (Hint: rhymes with "sock poaches")

7. *Fear Factor* challengers had to grab one of these many-toothed creatures by its tail; close cousin to a crocodile.

8. These creatures have a stinging tail and pinching claws; you wouldn't want to lay in a pit with a bunch of them, but *Fear Factor* players had to!

12. Baby houseflies; little squirmy things *Fear Factor* players had to put in their mouths. (Hint: rhymes with "agates")

14. Picking up these creatures proved to be a shocking experience for *Fear Factor* contestants. (Hint: second word rhymes with "heals") 2 words

DOWN

1. These jump around on your lawn — unless they're being eaten by *Fear Factor* contestants! Similar to locusts.

2. A very scary spider; it's big and hairy.

3. Contestants had to stick their faces into a fondue pot containing this. (Hint: rhymes with "oldie keys") 2 words

4. *Fear Factor* contestants had to use their mouths to pull these out of a tank of rats; they're at the base of the legs of a clucking farm animal (Hint: rhymes with "stickin' seat") 2 words

6. *Fear Factor* contestants had to swim with these dangerous little fish with sharp teeth. (Hint: their name sounds like "peer on, Oz")

9. Squids squirt this when they get scared; *Fear Factor* players had to drink it. (Hint: it's in your pen)

10. One of the gross ingredients of a *Fear Factor* pizza. (Hint: rhymes with "wish pies"; the first word is a creature that swims, the second word is what you see with) 2 words

11. In many stunts, players have to grab these that have *Fear Factor* written on them. (Hint: you pledge allegiance to one of these)

13. Playing with these flying insects was a *stinging* encounter; some make honey.

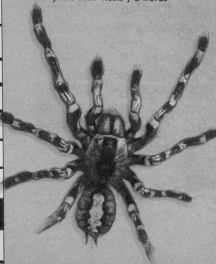

Answers on page 73

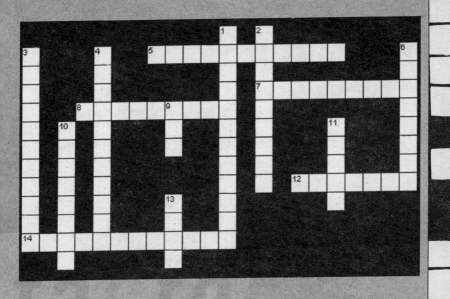

TERRIFYING TARANTULA
TRIVIA QUIZ!

CAN YOU UNTANGLE THESE QUESTIONS ABOUT OUR FUZZY, EIGHT-LEGGED FRIENDS?

Q: Tarantulas can grow to be as big as a . . .
a. Quarter
b. DVD
c. This book
d. Dinner plate

Answer: d, as big as a dinner plate. Scary!

Q: Which of the following is **NOT** true about tarantulas?
a. They have eight eyes.
b. They purposely harm **humans**.
c. They have no backbones.
d. People keep them as pets.

Answer: b, tarantulas never purposely harm humans, but will bite if threatened. The bite feels like a bad bee sting, and can cause an allergic reaction.

Q: How do tarantulas catch their prey?
a. They spin an enormous sticky web.
b. They bite it with their fangs.
c. They sting it with their tail.
d. They sing until it falls asleep, then smother it.

Answer: b, Ouch! Look out for those sharp teeth.

The PHobiC FaCt FiLe

ARACHNOPHOBIA IS THE FEAR OF SPIDERS!

Lots of people have arachnophobia, and many of them would be horrified to know that at any given time in most places, there's a spider within *six feet* of us! We hope it's not a female black widow—its poison is stronger than a rattlesnake's!

> ON *FEAR FACTOR*, CONTESTANTS HAVE TO LEAVE THEIR FEAR OF SPIDERS BEHIND!

THE EYES HAVE IT!

AN INTERVIEW WITH A CONTESTANT WHO ATE MORE THAN AN EYEFUL

FEAR FACTOR: What were you thinking when you saw all those eyes staring up at you?

CHARISSE: I glanced down and I looked back up right away when I saw those six eyeballs laying on the plate. I knew if I looked, I would gross myself out. I could not tell myself I was eating eyeballs, or it would not go down. So I said "cherries." Cherries was the word of the night.

FEAR FACTOR: So you thought "cherries" and then just dove right in?

CHARISSE: I just grabbed. I didn't care which one I grabbed. I just didn't want the biggest one. I grabbed the smallest one. I put it in my mouth, and I'm crying "cherries" in my brain. The first one popped in my mouth. I didn't breathe, because I didn't want to taste it. It just was gooshy and ooshy and crunchy. And I was pretty much praying. I was crossing my toes, you know, everything possible.

FEAR FACTOR: Was the first one the hardest to get down?

CHARISSE: As I started to swallow, I thought "eyeball" and I gagged. And that was, like, the scariest moment ever. I just started thinking "cherry, cherry, cherry, cherries." I think I said it a quatrillion times within a couple of seconds.

FEAR FACTOR: So eventually you got around to eating the big cow eye.

CHARISSE: The cow eye was just horrific. It just pops in your mouth. The juice went flying, and half the time it was coming out of my mouth. As I was chewing, I actually came up with a tactic. I had to swallow the juice first, then keep chewing on it to swallow the gooshy part. And then once I got to the main crunchy, hard part, I broke it down. And that was the only way I could do it.

FEAR FACTOR: Do you think you'll ever forget your *Fear Factor* eating experience?

CHARISSE: It was the most disgusting thing ever. I don't wish it upon anybody. Every time I eat now, I smell those eyeballs. It has not left me. I'm definitely traumatized. It's official!

The fear of eyes is called ommetaphobia or ommatophobia.

HOW ABOUT SOME
GROSS JOKES?

Q: What's worse than finding a worm in your apple?
A: *Finding half a worm!*

Q: Did you hear the joke about the moldy *Fear Factor* cheese?
A: *You don't want to. It stinks!*

Q: What's more gross? A *Fear Factor* stunt, or a really short guy who works in a supermarket?
A: *Well, the short guy is a little grocer.*

Q: What's the difference between a worm and a peach?
A: *Have you ever tried worm pie?*

Q: What's the most dangerous lunch is the world?
A: *A peanut butter and jellyfish sandwich!*

TOP TEN

Fear factor
GROSSEST STUNTS!

We assembled a panel of experts and asked them what stunts they thought were slimiest, grossest, and gooiest! Here are their choices. While it's not a list that's set in stone (after all, many of *Fear Factor's* grossest stunts are still to come), it is a pretty sick list! You can bet that each of these stunts rates a full **five stars** on *Fear Factor's* **Yuck-O-Meter**.

1. Maggot-and-Housefly Shake ★★★★★

The players met at a diner where the menu included a blended housefly-and-maggot shake. Players would have to transfer a gooey blended maggot mixture with their mouths into a shake glass filled with savory live flies. Once the glass was full, players would then have to drink the entire contents of the glass. The player who did this the slowest would be eliminated.

2. Doughnuts and Milk ★★★★★

At a doughnut shop, players had to eat some of the round treats with a hole in the middle. But these were not the kind of doughnuts that *anyone* would want to eat. One doughnut looked jelly filled but was actually filled with thick pig's blood. Another contained rotten squid and squid ink. The third variety had delectable, live stink beetles baked inside. And the fourth was filled with succulent, squirming worms. And what better to wash down *Fear Factor* doughnuts than with curdled milk? Players had to select two doughnuts, and if they were lucky, they'd get at least one of the five *real* jelly doughnuts hidden among the gross ones. Everyone who finished his or her doughnuts and milk would move on to the final round.

3. *Fear Factor* Pizza ★★★★★

The crust was made with smelly bile, straight from a cow's gallbladder, and topped with coagulated cow's blood paste and rancid cheese. Like at any fine pizzeria, players had their choice of toppings. Depending on what bucket they successfully tossed a pizza tray into, their slices would be topped either with succulent fish eyes, tangy live red worms, or a combination of the two. It's not delivery, it's *Fear Factor* pizza!

4. African Cave-Dwelling Spiders ★★★★★

In Las Vegas, players stood before a table full of African cave-dwelling spiders. The creatures looked like a cross between a spider and a long-legged crab. For each spider eaten, a player would receive two roulette chips. After eating the spiders, players would place their chips on the roulette board, and the wheel would be spun. If a player's chip was on the lucky number, that player would win a brand-new car! Quite an incentive to bite into a living, juicy spider!

5. Tomato Horn Worms ★★★★★

In head-to-head competitions, the players would have to chew up fat, squishy, green tomato horn worms and spit their guts into long narrow tubes until the tubes were full. Then they had to drink the guts cocktail. The three players who won their heats by choking down their glass of slimy worm guts the fastest would advance, while the other three would be eliminated.

6. Eating Madagascar Hissing Cockroaches ★★★★★

Fear Factor shuffleboard was used to determine how many roaches a player would have to eat, and it was anything but fun and games! Players would have one chance to push the shuffleboard disk into the scoring area. Whatever number the disk landed on (ranging from 0 to 5) would be the number of live, crunchy Madagascar hissing cockroaches they would have to eat. They also received a warning: the roaches' hard shells and spiny legs could damage players' windpipes, so it was important to chew them well! *Mmm-mmm!*

7. Cow Eyeballs ★★★★★

Out on a western ranch, contestants were shown a huge jar filled with cow eyeballs! Each player had to puncture the slick, rubbery eyeballs with their teeth and drain the pungent fluid into a nearby glass. Finally, they had to drink the cow eyeball juice. The players who completed the task the fastest would move on to the finals. Talk about looking a challenge right in the eye!

8. Rat Stew ★★★★★

In New York's Times Square, contestants were brought to a street vendor's cart—but hot dogs and pretzels weren't on the menu! A giant dead, decapitated rat was produced and thrown into a blender with some rat broth. The blender was activated, and fur, meat, and rat bones were quickly mixed into a chunky rat stew! Players competed to see who could drink down the disgusting batch the fastest. The one man and one woman who won their respective heats advanced to the finals. You better believe they were thinking, "Aw, rats!"

9. Spaghetti Made of Worms and Coagulated Blood ★★★★★

In a restaurant, *Fear Factor* revealed its version of spaghetti and meatballs: live night crawlers (worms) topped with blood meatballs. The blood meatballs were made of coagulated cow's blood wrapped in pig intestine. *Mama mia!*

10. Blended Banana Slugs and other Mixed Drinks ★★★★★

In Las Vegas, a waitress arrived with several hideous *Fear Factor* drink concoctions. One drink was made of blended Egyptian spiders and worms, another was made of cow's blood. There was one made with chewy scorpions, one of rotten fish eyes and eggs, and another of blended habanero peppers with tasty rattlesnake liver. Worst of all was the one made of gross banana slugs—with big, fat pieces of the slugs floating in it! *Eeeeeek!*

ANOTHER GUT-CHURNING CROSSWORD!

FILL IN THE BLANKS AND SOLVE PUKE-INDUCING PUZZLE #2:

ACROSS

2. Players had to drink shakes made from these hopping green amphibians. (Hint: rhymes with "full dogs")

3. On a beach, these spiderlike creatures were lunch for players. (Hint: rhymes with "land grabs") 2 words

4. Twin contestants had to gnaw the flesh off of these parts of a cow; bottom teeth are rooted in these. (Hint: rhymes with "law phones") 2 words

7. These organs are where a cow digests its food, and what players had to throw to one another.

9. In a fancy French restaurant, *Fear Factor* contestants ate these slimy bugs; they live in gardens and carry shells on their backs.

11. *Fear Factor* contestants had to lick three varieties of this insect off a rope. (Hint: their name sounds exactly like an old-time rock & roll band)

12. In a diner, contestants had to drink a shake made of maggots and these insects. (Hint: rhymes with "spies")

DOWN

1. Players fired a bazooka to determine how many of these ugly bugs they would have to chow down. (Hint: first word rhymes with "tomato") 2 words

5. Fill in the blank: African cave-dwelling _____; they're also called arachnids.

6. A particularly gruesome *Fear Factor* meal; animals run over by cars are called this. (Hint: rhymes with "toad pill") 2 words

8. Players had to crawl into a bag with hundreds of these insects, which rub their back legs together to make noise. (Hint: rhymes with "tickets")

10. These creatures grab onto your skin and suck your blood—*Fear Factor* players had to grab them with their mouths. (Hint: rhymes with "beaches")

Answers on page 74

PHOBIA QUESTIONS??

DON'T BE AFRAID! GO AHEAD AND TRY!

Q: What is the fear of dogs called?

a. Caninophobia

b. Puppaphobia

c. Cynophobia

d. Barkophobia

Answer: c. If you got that right, you're doggone smart!

Q: The fear of open space is called what?

a. Agoraphobia

b. Widophobia

c. Aerophobia

d. Vastophobia

Answer: a. Agoraphobics would hate walking on the moon!

Q: What is acrophobia the fear of?

a. Crossing streets

b. Akron, Ohio

c. Heights

d. Acorns and many other nuts

Answer: c. That's right—never look down!

- Producers of *Fear Factor* originally considered naming the show *Scared Stiff*, among other things.

- *Fear Factor* staff had to specially modify several blenders to blend tough, disgusting food items.

- Brave *Fear Factor* staff will perform the same stunts before the players have to—and do them several times to make sure they set appropriate rules for the stunts.

- Between stunts involving tarantulas, each individual spider has to be placed in a separate container to keep them from fighting with one another.

- When its cool, heaters are used to keep scorpions, rats, and frogs warm between stunts.

- More *Fear Factor* employees were bitten while working on a stunt with snakes and geckos than any other previous stunt.

The PHobiC FaCt FiLe
APIPHOBIA IS THE FEAR OF BEES!

Bees can fly fast, up to 22 miles per hour. No wonder apiphobes get nervous around them! Bees can also detect movement much faster than humans can, so it's hard to hide from them.

FEAR FACTOID

The stuff in a bee sting that hurts and itches is a chemical called mellitin.

ONE SET OF TWINS ON *FEAR FACTOR* WAS STUNG BY BEES MORE THAN THIRTY TIMES!

By the way, the fear of getting stung is cnidophobia.

TOP TEN

Fear factor
CREEPY STUNTS!

Besides being dangerous or gross, sometimes *Fear Factor* stunts are just plain creepy! What makes them creepy? Critters, that's what! Critters that slither, scamper, skitter, and crawl—usually all over players' bodies. And there's the critters with teeth that you normally wouldn't go swimming with for any amount of money. But *Fear Factor* players did! Here, then, are the cream of the crop of creepy stunts, each rating a maximum **five stars** on the *Fear Factor* **Creep-O-Meter:**

1. Family of Roaches ★★★★★
The stunt involved a parent and child. Each child was locked in a Plexiglas box filled with over 10,000 Madagascar hissing cockroaches. The parents transferred cockroaches (by mouth) to a scale, and when enough roaches were on the scale, a door opened to reveal a set of keys. The parents passed the keys to the children, who had to find the correct key to unlock themselves. The team that did this the fastest won a car and bikes. The cockroaches were heavy, smelly, and slimy—and more than one child looked like they were ready to give up, but they all pulled through!

2. Buzzing Bees ★★★★★
Teams of twins got a little buzzed during this stunt. One of them was covered in thousands of bees while shackled between two poles. The other twin had to search through a bee-filled stack of drawers to find the keys that would release the shackles and end the challenge.

3. 500 Tarantulas ★★★★★
This stunt was not only creepy, but it had a gross element, too. In a dark basement filled with cobwebs, women were strapped down in a coffin-shaped glass box, and more than 500 tarantulas were poured on top of them. The women's male partners would slurp up blended crickets and spit the mixture into a tube until a key floated to the top. The key was used to release a hacksaw, which was used to saw through a pipe, revealing a *Fear Factor* marker. Grabbing the marker would end the stunt and free the girls. But would they ever be free of the memory?

Fear factor
CREEPY STUNTS!

4. Piranha Tank ★★★★★

In Las Vegas, the *Fear Factor* crew revealed a large fish tank filled with more than 500 hungry piranhas! Scattered at the bottom of the tank were dozens of pig kidneys. Each player had to climb into the tank and retrieve seven of the pig kidneys by mouth. Under normal circumstances, a school of piranhas with their razor-sharp teeth can strip the flesh off a cow in a matter of a few minutes. Luckily, these piranhas didn't seem to be very hungry. But what if just a few decided they were ready for a snack? Ouch!

5. Scorpion Grave ★★★★★

Players arrived in a dark, wooded area where a shallow grave had been dug. Each contestant climbed into the grave, where they were covered with 3,000 pinching, biting, poisonous scorpions! Then, while they were covered in these notoriously unsociable creatures, each player had to maneuver a joystick to grab scorpions with a robotic arm and transfer them into an adjoining pit. The two players who transferred the most scorpions won. You could probably hear the players screaming from a block away!

6. Boas and Pythons and Geckos—Oh, My! ★★★★★

Snakes and lizards! Two competing players climbed into a large, clear box with a mixture of more than 600 boa constrictors, pythons, and geckos! There was just enough room for two humans, who raced to slide metal disks from the bottom of the box to the top of the wall. The first player to successfully transfer five disks would win. But there were no guarantees against snake bites!

7. Electric Eel Transfer ★★★★★

An electric eel contains about 650 volts of electricity! Players had to transfer six of these eels from one side of a tank to the other, using only one hand. Grabbing an eel with two hands would risk getting a deadly zap. Needless to say, it was a shocking experience!

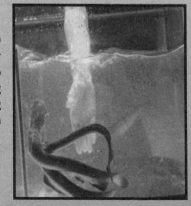

8. Swimming with Alligators ★★★★

For this stunt, there was a giant fish tank—filled with alligators. The gators had razor-sharp teeth. The players, of course, watched the gators for only one quick moment, then hastily scampered away, right? Wrong! They each had to slide into the tank and retrieve three poles from the bottom. They had to transfer the poles to a rack alongside the tank one at a time. The two who completed the stunt the fastest moved on to the final round. They were all pretty fast, though, because they were each thinking two little words: gator bait!

9. Bullfrog, Scorpion, and Rat Race ★★★★★

Here was another gross/creepy challenge! Female partners were locked in a sunken pit with a bamboo gate, which was then filled with live bullfrogs. The men had to run across the swamp and fish out a key from a pit filled with scorpions, run back and undo the first lock, and then cross back through the swamp to a pit filled with rats to get a second key. And they had to retrieve these keys using only their mouths! Once they freed their partners, the duos raced back to drink their frog shake. That's right, a gross, blended, bullfrog-and-swamp-water-shake! *Ugh!*

10. Leech Coffin ★★★★★

In this stunt, a waterproof Plexiglas coffin was filled with blood-sucking leeches. Each player had to pump water out of the coffin for as long as possible, while the leeches suctioned onto their skin. The two contestants who lasted the longest advanced to the next round.

WORD SEARCH 1:

GROSS AND SICK WORD SEARCH!

FIND AND CIRCLE THE WORDS BELOW TO DISCOVER

THE SECRET MESSAGE:

PUZZLE WORDS

BILE	SLIME
BOBBING	SNAKES
CONTESTANT	STEW
DISGUST	VENOM
INSECTS	WINNER
RATS	WORM
SICKENING	

Once you've completed the Word Search, circle the first 15 letters to reveal the secret message.

Answers on page 77

C	O	N	T	E	S	T	A	N	T
W	W	A	I	T	C	H	F	S	R
E	E	S	A	N	R	W	I	F	A
T	A	R	E	M	S	C	O	C	T
S	T	E	O	K	K	E	O	R	S
R	F	N	Y	E	A	L	C	V	M
P	E	N	N	N	E	N	T	T	V
V	M	I	W	L	K	J	S	T	S
T	N	W	I	M	E	M	I	L	S
G	J	B	O	B	B	I	N	G	N
W	D	I	S	G	U	S	T	Y	N

The PHobiC FaCt File

SCOLECIPHOBIA IS THE FEAR OF WORMS!

There are 3,000 species of worms, and there can be anywhere between 500,000 and a million worms per acre of land. A farmer with scoleciphobia would have a hard time doing his job! But worms, through their actions, substantially change dirt and soil. They alter its composition, increase its capacity to absorb and hold water, and bring about an increase in nutrients and microorganisms. In short, they prepare the soil for farming!

SCOLECIPHOBES WOULDN'T LIKE *FEAR FACTOR*'S SPAGHETTI & MEATBALL CHALLENGE— PLAYERS HAD TO EAT WORMS COVERED WITH DIRT!

By the way, the fear of filth or dirt is rupophobia.

DID YOU KNOW . . . ?

- A leech is a worm that feeds on blood. It pierces its victim's skin and fills itself with three to four times its own body weight in blood. *Talk about pigging out!*

- A cockroach can live for up to a week without its head. *Yeah, but would it really enjoy itself?*

- In Korea, some people eat Poshintang (dog meat soup!). A popular item on summertime menus, it is believed to cure summer heat ailments and improve women's complexions.

- Rats are omnivorous, eating nearly any type of food, including other rats that are dead or dying! *What are friends for?*

- After eating, a housefly barfs up its food, then gobbles it up again. *Oh, boy, seconds!*

- When mother hamsters have a lot of babies, sometimes they'll eat a few of them to keep the population down. *Thanks a lot, Mom!*

WARTS AND ALL!

AN INTERVIEW WITH A DYNAMIC DUO, WHO SUFFERED A PLAGUE OF FROGS

FEAR FACTOR: So, were you scared about having a hundred giant bullfrogs dumped on you?

MARIA: I was kind of freaked out about getting warts. They say that if you kiss 'em, they'll give you warts. But I stopped thinking about that as soon as they poured them on me. All of a sudden, you have hundreds of these little cold slimy bodies climbing around on you. It's just really weird. The whole coffin was a cage filled with frogs. They don't just dump them on your body, they dump them right on your head so they were all over my face. Nobody wants to sit in a tank with frogs and cold water. It's not a fun thing to do.

FEAR FACTOR: After Craig had retrieved the keys from the scorpions and rats and freed you, the two of you had to suck down a blended bullfrog shake. What was that like?

MARIA: I immediately went back to the shake we drank on top of the building. I'm thinking, okay, that took 30 seconds. This one will be like a minute. It'll probably be a little chunkier, but we'll get through it. No big deal. I couldn't have been more wrong. The first sip just tasted like barf—barf mixed with swamp water.

CRAIG: It was bones and eyes and feet and just everything. The frog wouldn't even blend. They needed a special blender to blend that thing 'cause of all the bones. It was nasty. You could feel every chunk clawing its way down your throat and sliding to the bottom of your stomach. It was just nasty.

MARIA: Frogs don't really have claws, so it must've been their bones or whatever, but every single gulp was scratching your throat the whole way down. There are probably cuts on our throats.

CRAIG: One thing is for sure, these stunts aren't getting any easier.

HOLIDAYS THE *FEAR FACTOR* WAY!

When folks get together for any holiday event, it's usually a time of joyous celebration, of reconnecting with family and friends, and mostly, it's about being served great food. But not on *Fear Factor*! Observe these stunts of holidays past.

SWIMMING WITH SNAKES FOR HALLOWEEN 2003

Players reclined in a coffin-size tank, filled with 400 gallons of water. Their hands and feet were handcuffed. Three separate keys were dropped into the water, along with hundreds of writhing, slithering snakes! Each player had to find the keys, free themselves, and grab a nearby *Fear Factor* flag while literally swimming in snakes! **CREEP-O-METER RATING ★★★**

EXCHANGING GRUESOME GIFTS FOR CHRISTMAS 2003

To celebrate the Yuletide season, players took part in a traditional holiday gift exchange—with a *Fear Factor* twist! In brightly wrapped boxes underneath a sparkling tree were some of the most disgusting things in *Fear Factor* history. One player would choose a box and reveal its edible contents. The next player could either "steal" whatever the first player chose or get something of their own, and so on until everyone had a treat to eat. These included an icky cod egg sack covered in ants, a yummy live worm sausage (sausage casing stuffed with live red worms, earthworms, and super worms), live dragonflies, and a jar filled with six rotten squid covered in live flies! **YUCK-O-METER RATING ★★★★★**

SPECIAL WITCH'S BREW FOR HALLOWEEN 2004

On an eerie set, contestants were led to a bubbling cauldron. Inside was a boiling broth with juicy bits of scorpions and tarantulas! Each player had to consume some brew, depending on how well they completed a competition with a crossbow. They shot flaming arrows at a scarecrow, and the number of shots it took to ignite the scarecrow dictated how many cups of brew they had to consume. YUCK-O-METER RATING ★★★★

A ROTTING FEAST FOR THANKSGIVING 2004

Just like the pilgrims who arrived at Plymouth Rock, players got a chance to sit down to a nice Thanksgiving feast—with a slight *Fear Factor* twist! With a rotting, maggot-infested turkey as the table's centerpiece, players had to choose three out of five mystery side dishes to chow down. For each side dish they consumed, they got a chance to throw a hatchet at a nearby target. The contestant who got closest to the bull's-eye won some major bucks and a video-game console. Pretty sweet—which is more than can be said of the mystery side dishes! They all had to pile their plates high with thick worm green beans; maggoty mashed potatoes with rotten fish sauce gravy; bile gelatin topped with live African cave-dwelling spiders; beetle, worm, and cockroach stuffing; and for dessert, sheep's brain pie. Be thankful *you* didn't have to eat it! YUCK-O-METER RATING ★★★★★

HORRIFYING HOLIDAY CHEER FOR CHRISTMAS 2004

In a cozy snow-covered cabin, hung by the chimney with care, were Christmas stockings marked with each player's name. In each player's stocking were gift boxes. Each gift box contained a number that corresponded to the number of reindeer parts the contestants had to eat. That's right, reindeer. Each player would have to eat between five and ten reindeer innards. And what holiday treat would be complete without a little eggnog? Not the sweet, creamy stuff you're used to, but eggnog made from *hundred-year-old* eggs. It had the consistency and color of pureed guacamole. Nothing says "ho, ho, ho!" like reindeer bits and a moldy, chunky, smelly glass of eggnog! YUCK-O-METER RATING ★★★

STRAIGHT FROM A PLAYER'S MOUTH!

AN INTERVIEW WITH A HOLIDAY SURVIVOR

FEAR FACTOR: What was the worst dish in your *Fear Factor* Thanksgiving feast?

JAYSON: The gelatin parts with the spiders were the worst. I don't even know what that was. It tasted like raw sewage and cat urine mixed with ecto-slime, and I don't even know what that is. It immediately wanted to come back up after I ate it.

FEAR FACTOR: What about the worms?

JAYSON: The first time I felt the worm in my mouth, it was just beyond horrible. I bit into it and it was just mushy and chewy and it wouldn't go down. It just sat in my throat. It was like gum; I couldn't break it down. It was the most ridiculous thing, ever. I was trying to swallow them as much as I could and I realized, the more I tried to swallow it, the more it would try and wiggle its way back up. So I just decided to not touch the worms at all, and move on to the beetles.

FEAR FACTOR: How were they?

JAYSON: As soon as I put the beetles in my mouth, they started walking on my tongue. It felt like one of them was doing the moonwalk. I could feel it tickling and going backward. I tried biting it and it was just so nasty to feel those needlelike legs all over my tongue. It was disgusting.

The PHobiC FaCt FiLe

OPHIDIOPHOBIA IS THE FEAR OF SNAKES!

Fear of snakes is the most common of phobias. Even some monkeys have it! And it's no wonder, since snakes can be so silent and dangerous. Did you know that some snakes will eat other snakes? Lucky for them, snakes are immune to their own poison. There were several incidents of crew members being bit when snakes were on *Fear Factor*!

OPHIDIOPHOBES WOULDN'T CRAWL INTO A TANK FULL OF SNAKES ON *FEAR FACTOR*!

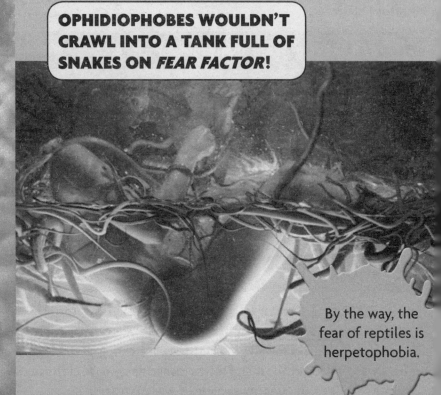

By the way, the fear of reptiles is herpetophobia.

SNAKE
TRIVIA QUIZ!

Q: **Which sense do snakes use the least?**

a. Scent

b. Vision

c. Heat detection

d. Feeling vibrations

Answer: a. Which explains why they never buy underarm deodorant!

Q: **Which type of snake is the heaviest, weighing over 300 pounds?**

a. Reticulated python

b. Indian python

c. Monty python

d. Green anaconda

Answer: d. No wonder it's green—it envies slimmer snakes!

Q: **Which is *not* one of the ways a snake moves?**

a. Concertina movement

b. Rectilinear movement

c. Shuffle movement

d. Sidewinder movement

Answer: c. Rectilinear movement is what a caterpillar uses.

CROSSWORD CRAZINESS RETURNS!

FILL IN THE BLANKS AND SOLVE UNPALATABLE PUZZLE #3:

ACROSS

2. This insect was named after a mythical flying beast that breathes fire.

3. Players had to get up close and personal with these really long snakes; they squeeze their victims. (Hint: first word rhymes with "Noah") 2 words

6. On one episode, players had to drink a glass of this spoiled beverage. (Hint: you put it on cereal)

7. These little lizards like to crawl all over *Fear Factor* players and bite them. (Hint: rhymes with "echoes")

9. Using only their mouths, contestants had to fill a crate with these wiggly creatures; they live in soil and crawl out when it rains.

11. Fill in the blank: _____ horse grasshoppers. (Hint: it means "really big")

DOWN

1. Eating these didn't necessarily make *Fear Factor* players smarter, but without them, cows would be really dumb! 2 words

2. A pie made with something from the mouths of these quacking birds was another *Fear Factor* treat to eat. (Hint: the first word rhymes with "yuck," second word is what your doctor will ask you to stick out before you say "ahhh") 2 words

4. On *Fear Factor*, this classic Italian meal was made from blobs of cow's blood and worms, instead of meatballs and noodles.

5. According to *Fear Factor* contestants, the worst part of most gross stunts is the what? (Hint: rhymes with "tell")

8. During a Christmas show, one player got a "present" to eat made of a cod egg sack covered with these little insects. (Hint: rhymes with "pants")

10. These bugs have a name that means "one thousand feet," and you can bet these wormy critters were using every one of those legs to get away from contestants' mouths! (Hint: rhymes with "fill a beads")

Answers on page 75

DID YOU KNOW . . . ?

- In one stunt, each contestant had more than *thirty gallons* of squid ink dumped over their heads. *Brings new meaning to the phrase "inking the deal"!*

- *Fear Factor* producers use pigs' tongues in stunts because of their close resemblance to the human tongue. *In this case, I don't think the familiarity is comforting!*

- The rats eaten in a New York City stunt were flown in from California. *How thoughtful!*

- In the challenge where contestants had to lick live bugs off ropes, a special concoction of rotten fish and blended worms was developed to flavor the edible adhesive used to secure the bugs to the ropes. *Bet that meal really stuck to their ribs!*

- African tree boa constrictors used in a season-five stunt were incredibly aggressive and bit both the contestants and the snake wranglers dozens of times. *Maybe they were camera shy!*

- The taste of blended night crawler worms has been described as like "vomit with a hint of dirt." *What a delightful bouquet!*

- All "foods" seen eaten on the show have to be FDA approved. *USDA recommended cow brains?*

MORE STARTLING STATISTICS!

RECORDS FOR SOME UNUSUALLY
GROSS *FEAR FACTOR* STUNTS

• Fastest time for a couples stunt, in which the women had to spit mouthfuls of jet-black squid ink pouring from a basin back into the guys' mouths so that the guys could spit it into a cylinder until it was full: 1 minute, 22 seconds.

YUCK-O-METER RATING ★★★

• Best time for a challenge in which one sibling passed a key to the other by mouth, and the sibling who received the key dropped it through a slot, grabbed it, and unlocked the both of them (all while their heads were trapped in web-laden Plexiglas boxes filled with tarantulas and other spiders, of course!): 1 minute, 0.3 seconds.

CREEP-O-METER RATING ★★★★

• Most weight of worms, cockroaches, and three kinds of beetles licked off of a rope and transferred to a bowl in a one-minute time period: 203.2 grams. **YUCK-O-METER RATING ★★★★**

• **Most** leeches transferred by mouth from a tank to a bowl by a team of best friends: 200 leeches.

YUCK-O-METER RATING ★★★★

• Record time for a couples team who worked together to transfer big, slippery tunas from one end of a tank filled with rancid water and fish parts to the other, then dived under to retrieve and consume one of four *Fear Factor* delicacies (cod egg sack, fish eyes, fish stomach, or sea snails): 5 minutes, 18 seconds.

YUCK-O-METER RATING ★★★★

✔ ASKED & ANSWERED!

WE ASKED PLAYERS, WHAT WOULD YOUR FRIENDS SAY ARE YOUR WORST QUALITIES? HERE'S WHAT THEY SAID:

✔ "That I'm very competitive and hate to be wrong."

✔ "I'm too aggressive and competitive."

✔ "I have a big mouth and always speak my mind."

✔ "I hold things in until I finally explode. And my friends are like, 'Where did that come from?'"

✔ "I always, always, always want all of my friends to hang out. Now, if you're tired or just don't want to do anything, I'm your biggest nightmare. I'm a nag, I guess I would say. I usually don't stop until they break down and come out."

✔ "I'm a little naive and stubborn."

✔ "That I'm honest. For example, I'll say, 'Yes, you need to lose five pounds.'"

✔ "I love to argue. I always think that I am right, and most of the time, I am. My mouth speaks faster than my brain thinks and it tends to get me into trouble."

CREEPY COCKROACH CORNER!

INTERESTING TRIVIA ABOUT ONE OF EARTH'S LOWLIEST CREATURES

- As mentioned earlier, a cockroach can live a week without its head. It would live longer, but it can't drink water and dies of thirst. *Headless and thirsty is no way to go through life, son!*

- Cockroaches bleed white blood. *As evidenced when* Fear Factor *players bite into them! Ewww!*

- Crushed cockroaches can be applied to a stinging wound and help relieve the pain. *Your pain, that is, not the cockroach's!*

- Roaches can live without food for a month but will survive only a week without water. *Kind of like a camel—only opposite!*

- A cockroach heart is nothing but a simple tube with valves pumping blood backward and forward. Its heart can even stop moving without harming the roach. *Efficient! Do they come with fuel injection?*

- Cockroaches can climb walls because they are equipped with a set of little claws on their feet. *Actually, Cockroach-Man would be a pretty neat superhero!*

CRAWLING, CREEPING, LEAPING, AND SWIMMING!

A QUICK TRIVIA QUIZ!
ABOUT REPTILES AND AMPHIBIANS

Q: What is the largest snake in the Western hemisphere?

a. King snake
b. Boa constrictor
c. Anaconda
d. Black mamba

Answer: c. You couldn't have missed this one—there was a movie about it!

Q: The Egyptian cobra is known by what other name?

a. Nileskipper
b. Viper
c. Basket weaver
d. Asp

Answer: d. Do they like that name? Go ahead and asp them!

Q: The largest reptile in North America is what?

a. Sea turtle
b. Alligator
c. Cincinnati caiman
d. Mammoth iguana

Answer: b. Luckily, most of them stay in the swamps!

STRAIGHT FROM A PLAYER'S MOUTH!

AN INTERVIEW WITH A CONTESTANT WHO REMOVED BUGS FROM A ROPE LICKETY-SPLIT!

FEAR FACTOR: What did you think when you first saw the stunt?

KATE: When I first saw the stunt, I just couldn't believe it. I thought it was the funniest thing that I've ever heard of people having to do, so I just could not stop laughing. And then when it came to be my turn, I stopped laughing. That's for sure. The odor really, really gets to you, so I was trying not to breathe through my nose at all.

FEAR FACTOR: What was your strategy?

KATE: To be as quick as possible in getting them in my mouth and over to the scales. I just wanted to move quick, just get a mouthful and move as quick as I could to the scales. I was looking for the biggest globs of bugs that I could get into my mouth.

FEAR FACTOR: What technique did you use for getting the bugs off of the ropes?

KATE: I just took my mouth from the bottom of the rope and was going upward to just try and gather as many as I could in my mouth. It was disgusting, but I had to do what I had to do.

FEAR FACTOR: Was it sticky?

KATE: Yeah, it was really sticky. And it stank. It was horrid.

FEAR FACTOR: How gross were the bugs? How did they feel in your mouth?

KATE: It was disgusting. I tried to block it out of my mind and just get as many in my mouth as I could and spit them into that bowl as quick as I could. I was trying to put saliva around my lips before I started 'cause I thought that would stop them from biting me. But today I've got lots of little blisters on the top and bottom of my lip from those little buggers biting away. When it was all over, I just felt repulsively ill. It was disgusting. And I'm sure everyone's gonna have a good laugh with those bugs smeared all over my face. It was disgusting.

41

The PHobiC FaCt FiLe
ENTOMOPHOBIA IS THE FEAR OF INSECTS!

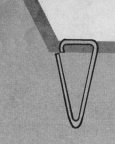

Insects are a useful source of protein in some parts of the world. For example, dried locusts are 75% protein and 20% fat, and contain several vitamins. The question is, would entomophobes catch and eat insects if they were starving?

MADAGASCAR HISSING COCKROACHES ARE *FEAR FACTOR*'S FAVORITE INSECT!

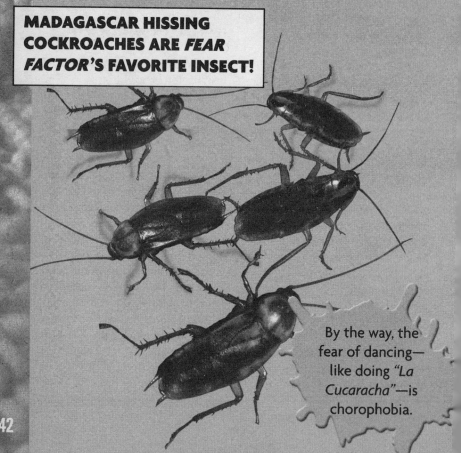

By the way, the fear of dancing—like doing *"La Cucaracha"*—is chorophobia.

ALTERNATIVE TERRORS!

On *Fear Factor*, the producers usually reserve day two of an episode for the gross or creepy stunts, like the ones we've focused on in this book. Every once in a while, those wily producers throw the players a curve ball and bring out an altogether different kind of horrific challenge. These were some of the best.

What a Gas

Unlike the typical second stunt, it was broad daylight and players didn't have to eat anything or have anything crawl on them. They were at a Chemical Agents Training Office and had to survive a lung-searing, eyeball-melting, tear-gassing! One by one, the players entered the facility to see how long they could last in a gas-filled chamber. The three contestants who lasted the longest before hitting a release button advanced to the next round.

YUCK-O-METER RATING ★
GAG-O-METER RATING ★★★★★

Walking on Broken Glass

In an abandoned warehouse, players learned that they each would throw rocks at a set of glass panels marked with numbers ranging from five to ten. The number they hit represented the number of feet they would walk, barefoot, over shards of broken glass!

YUCK-O-METER RATING ★★
CRINGE-O-METER RATING ★★★★★

Swampy Gator

On an all-women show, players had to wade through the swamp, gathering keys. The first key was in the water. The second key was in an old rowboat. And the third was up a tree. Next, the players had to find the right key to unlock a gated tunnel. Finally, they had to pull an 8-foot-long, 400-pound alligator out of the tunnel by its tail!

YUCK-O-METER RATING ★
YIKES!-O-METER RATING ★★★★

The Shocking Maze

Couples arrived at a power plant and got the shock of their lives: This stunt would send powerful volts of electricity into their bodies! The couples were handcuffed while they navigated through an electrically charged maze of tangled wires to retrieve *Fear Factor* flags. Each time they touched a wire within the maze, they'd be hit with painful volts of electricity!

YUCK-O-METER RATING ★
ZZZAP-O-METER RATING ★★★★

Lard Almighty!

This was during a parent-child teams episode. To win, the teams had to crawl through thousands of pounds of pig lard and pig parts! The kids had to grab a cow tongue out of a bucket, then crawl to the center of the tunnel and hand off the tongue to their parents. The parents had to crawl out their end of the lard and place the tongue in another bucket. The team that transferred seven tongues the fastest won a fabulous trip.

YUCK-O-METER RATING ★★★
SLIP 'N' SLIDE-O-METER RATING ★★★★

Raw Sewage

This couples stunt involved side-by-side Dumpsters filled with trash. Long, narrow, clear chutes led into each Dumpster. Each guy sat beneath the chute, handcuffed to the outside, popping their heads up inside the chute. As tons of raw sewage was pumped down the chute at their faces, their partners had to navigate the rapidly filling Dumpster, crawl up the narrow chute, and retrieve the key to the cuffs. Once back outside the chute, the girls would free their partners. The first guy to release a *Fear Factor* flag from the edge of the Dumpster won the heat for his team.

YUCK-O-METER RATING ★★★★★
PLUS AN EXTRA ★★!

- McNasty, an alligator featured in a swamp stunt where players had to grab him by the tail, is known for his extremely bad attitude. *You would have a bad attitude, too, if strangers were yanking your tail!*

- For the stunt where players had to lick bugs off of a car's windshield, rubber mallets and an air cannon were used by crew members to smash the already-dead bugs onto the windshield. *"If I had a hammer . . ."*

- A pack of wild coyotes was attracted to the smell of rotting cow parts during the filming of the Gross Dunk Tank stunt. *They better stay away—they could end up on the next* Fear Factor *menu!*

- When bees covered contestants in a stunt featuring twins, the combined weight of the bees was almost 20 pounds. *"Do these bees make me look fat?"*

- The protein content of a cow brain is slightly less than that of a T-bone steak. *I'll stick with the steak, thanks.*

- The average lifespan of a Madagascar hissing cockroach is 2.5 years. *That's a lot of nights rummaging through people's kitchens!*

WORD SEARCH 2:

ANOTHER SICKENING WORD SEARCH!

FIND AND CIRCLE THE WORDS BELOW TO DISCOVER

THE SECRET MESSAGE:

PUZZLE WORDS

BLOOD	GROSS
CHAMPION	HEART
COFFIN	SLOP
COMPETE	SLURP
CREEPY	SPIDERS
CRUNCHY	SQUIRMY
GAGGING	

Once you've solved the word search, the first 16 uncircled letters spell out the message.

Answers on page 77

P	O	C	O	F	F	I	N	T	A	T
O	B	S	Q	U	I	R	M	Y	U	G
B	A	S	Z	G	O	G	H	O	K	A
Z	N	K	P	B	N	E	R	D	G	E
T	O	B	K	I	A	I	O	O	T	K
X	I	F	T	R	D	O	G	E	S	V
Q	P	P	T	Z	L	E	P	G	J	S
O	M	R	K	B	B	M	R	T	A	H
P	A	U	B	P	O	L	S	S	K	G
G	H	L	X	C	Y	P	E	E	R	C
N	C	S	C	R	U	N	C	H	Y	N

A SHATTERING EXPERIENCE!

AN INTERVIEW WITH A PLAYER WHO
TOOK PAINFUL STEPS ... ON BROKEN GLASS

FEAR FACTOR: Was this stunt at all what you were expecting?

DERRICK: No. When I saw the stunt, my heart dropped. It completely dropped to my stomach and I'm like, "God, I cannot believe I have to walk across glass. Really, Derrick, what have you got yourself into?" I figured it was going to be something to eat. I was thinking something gross. I was not expecting glass whatsoever.

FEAR FACTOR: What were you thinking as you were preparing to walk on all those shards of glass?

DERRICK: I was looking at the glass and saying, "God, I do not want to cut my feet up. I really do not want to mess my feet up." I knew I was going to have to get through it, I want this money so bad. I want this fifty grand. Fifty thousand dollars could do so much for me right now. It's just a matter of sucking it up and doing it, pain or no pain.

FEAR FACTOR: So what is your tolerance level for pain?

DERRICK: On a scale of one to ten, my pain tolerance is negative five. I'm not a pain person at all. I'm not a crybaby or anything, I rarely shed a tear, but when I saw that glass, I just figured I was going to start bawling, walking across the glass.

FEAR FACTOR: What was your first step like?

DERRICK: I think I had every muscle in my foot as tight as it possibly could be. Thank God I'm flatfooted. So I just flattened my feet and tightened up every muscle and took that first step. It was really difficult, because you didn't want to push your weight on your foot to go too far on the glass.

FEAR FACT

The "*Fear Factor* maggots" are actually mealworms. They're easier to get in large quantities, and more importantly— they're bigger!

This revolting recipe is a closely guarded secret—and, frankly, we don't want to know what's in it!

FEAR FACT

In this stunt, one of the players got an allergic reaction just from reaching into the fish—making her (not pictured) the only contestant ever to be excused from a stunt due to allergy.

Luckily, *Fear Factor* always has medical staff on hand.

FEAR FACT

The cheeses used for this stunt smell so disgusting that they're the only gross food to be banned from the *Fear Factor* offices.

FEAR FACT

Because of mad cow disease, cow brains are no longer used on *Fear Factor*. But don't worry—there's still plenty of sheep brains to fill the gross void!

FEAR FACT

Everyone agrees that the maggot-and-house-fly shake was probably the grossest challenge ever seen on *Fear Factor*.

Ever wonder how the crew managed to get all those live flies into a glass? It's a simple trick: They put the flies into the freezer for exactly three minutes to slow them down; then, once the flies thawed out, they were buzzing around again—trapped inside the glass.

FEAR FACTOR: What physically happens to you when you walk on the glass?

DERRICK: My back and the bottom of my feet were dripping in sweat. Just pouring sweat, and I didn't even think my feet sweat, but they were dripping.

FEAR FACTOR: We noticed at times that you picked up your foot and tried to brush off the glass. What was that strategy all about?

DERRICK: When I felt the glass on the bottom of my foot, I had to wipe it off—I did not want to get cut walking across this glass.

FEAR FACTOR: Were you worried about losing your balance?

DERRICK: No, I'm a pretty good balancer. I've never done tightrope or balancing beam or anything like that, but I'm a pretty good balancer. The only thing I was afraid of by picking up one foot, and it just went through my head for one second, was, "Derrick, what are you doing? You're going to fall on your face and you're going to mess your face all up and have hundreds and hundreds of cuts all over your face and your body." And that's just the one thing I don't want to mess up is my face. I do not want to cut my face. I'd rather cut the bottom of my feet than my face.

FEAR FACTOR: You and the other contestants played a game to determine whether you'd have to walk anywhere from 5 to 10 feet of broken glass. Do you think it's a big advantage to only have to walk five feet?

DERRICK: Five feet seems like a mile when it's just hundreds and hundreds and hundreds of pieces of broken glass.

THERE'S NO BUSINESS LIKE CREEPY, GROSS BUSINESS!

The celebrity editions of *Fear Factor* featured some of the most memorable stunts ever seen on the show. So, here's some of the grossest and/or creepiest! If you watched the episodes these stunts were in, you might fondly remember the exploits of certain celebrities. If you didn't watch, just imagine some of your favorite music, TV, or movie stars doing this stuff!

Backward Slide of Grossness

Each player had to slide backward through a narrow tube to retrieve three keys while gushing water blasted at them. Each time they grabbed a key, 50 gallons of either fish guts, fish oil, or worms dumped onto them. Ultimately, the players used the collected keys to open the escape hatch and finish the stunt. After the second key was pulled, the water hose stopped—leaving slimy guts, oil, and worms for them to swim through. YUCK-O-METER RATING ★★★

Handcuffs of Horror

Players had one hand handcuffed to a bar that ran the length of a long table. On the table were several items. The first item was a box they had to reach into and take apart a puzzle to get a key. Unfortunately, the box was filled with biting, snapping, ornery Amazon tree boa constrictors! Then they moved to another box, filled with giant, slimy, SMELLY worms, and unlocked it with the key. Each player had to transfer worms twice by mouth, filling a blender with the squirmy fellows. Next, they had to suck the fresh-blended worm juice out of the blender to fill a cylinder. As the cylinder filled, it brought the handcuff key to the top. Players used the blender key to release themselves from the bar, then jumped into a huge Dumpster of even more big, fat, stinky worms. Hidden in the Dumpster was a canister filled with more worm guts and sludge. Each contestant had to drink these disgusting contents before the stunt was considered finished. *Whew!* YUCK-O-METER RATING ★★★★★

Golfing for Grossness

Players met at a dark and creepy miniature golf course for some golfing—*Fear Factor* style! Each celebrity would have to sink one ball. The more strokes they took, the larger the slimy sea cucumber they'd have to eat. Five or more strokes meant the player ate the biggest sea cucumber, while a hole-in-one meant no cucumber at all! Sea cucumbers are exceedingly slimy and gross!

YUCK-O-METER RATING ★★★★

Guts of Glory

Contestants gathered near a tank filled with 5,000 pounds of stinking, rotting, disgusting fish scales. The liquid was a milky gray color and smelled as bad as it looked. At the bottom of the tank were eight thermoses, one of which contained fermented squid guts. After locating the gut-filled thermos, each player had to drink one glass of the guts!

YUCK-O-METER RATING ★★★★★

The Torment Cell

The celebrity players tramped through a graffiti-laden, trash-strewn abandoned subway tunnel in downtown Los Angeles to reach the Torment Cell. A small Plexiglas box was positioned so that each player could easily stick their heads up into it. Once inside, the stars shared the small space with super worms, millipedes, and 20 Emperor scorpions! Within seconds, players were literally up to their eyeballs in smelly, biting, stinging creepy-crawlies. They had to endure three minutes of worms up their noses and in their ears and hair!

CREEP-O-METER RATING ★★★★

Hockey Pucks of Peril

At the bottom of the glass aquarium-like tank were 1,000 hockey pucks, 100 of which were painted yellow on one side. Players had to retrieve as many yellow pucks as possible in 90 seconds. But, besides the hockey pucks, there were also snakes—a 10-foot albino Burmese python would be swimming with them, and he brought 1,000 little snake friends along for the fun!

CREEP-O-METER RATING ★ ★ ★ ★

Fear Factor Fruit Flies

In a Plexiglas box, a dozen strawberries hung delicately from strings. Each celeb contestant had to stick their head in the box and eat as many strawberries as possible in two minutes. Those who ate them all in the allotted time automatically advanced. No problem, right? The problem was, that box was also filled with thousands of pesky flies! They couldn't take a bite of a strawberry without scarfing down a few flies, too!

YUCK-O-METER RATING ★ ★ ★ ★

Coffin Times Three

Each player had to lay down in a Plexiglas coffin that was separated into three sections. From the knees down, players' bare legs (they all had to wear shorts) were covered in thousands of night crawler worms. Their midsections were swarming in red and white snakes. And their heads were surrounded by 3,000 gigantic Madagascar hissing cockroaches! Plexiglas dividers kept each section separate, while players sorted out the white snakes from the red ones in this creepy timed event.

CREEP-O-METER RATING ★ ★ ★ ★ ★

TRIVIA QUIZ!

~~ABOUT~~ GRASSHOPPERS

Grasshoppers are sometimes a tasty meal on *Fear Factor*, but how much do you really know about them?

Q: **How far can grasshoppers leap?**
- a. 5 times their length
- b. 10 times their length
- c. 15 times their length
- d. 20 times their length

Answer: d. If humans could leap 20 times our body size, we'd be able to jump almost 40 yards, nearly half a football field!

Q: **What do 3 ounces of grasshoppers have when compared with 3 ounces of steak?**
- a. More protein
- b. More fat
- c. More sodium
- d. More oil

Answer: a. Yummy! Grasshoppers have 300% more protein than steak does!

Q: **In some parts of the world, grasshoppers are eaten after being . . .**
- a. Ground into meal
- b. Dipped in honey
- c. Jellied
- d. Covered in chocolate

Answer: Trick question! All answers are correct!

DID YOU KNOW...?

- Each year, rodents cause more than one billion dollars in damage in the United States alone. *The truth is clear—they make lousy house guests!*

- Rats memorize specific pathways and use the same routes habitually. *As creatures of habit, they're probably terribly boring to travel with!*

- Rats can get into your home through a hole about the size of a quarter. *We need smaller holes or bigger quarters!*

- These rodents rely predominantly on smell, taste, touch, and hearing as opposed to vision. *Even the Invisible Man would have trouble sneaking up on them!*

- They move around mainly in the dark, using their long, sensitive whiskers and the guard hairs on their body to guide them. *Give 'em all haircuts, I say!*

- Rats constantly gnaw anything softer than their own teeth, including lead sheeting, improperly cured concrete, sun-dried adobe brick, cinderblock, wood, and aluminum sheeting. *Why can't they stick to potato chips, like the rest of us?*

- A rat can drop down 50 feet without injury. *But that last inch can still be painful!*

The Phobic Fact File

MUSOPHOBIA IS THE FEAR OF RATS!

There are two primary types of rats in the United States—Norway rats and roof rats. Water doesn't stop Norway rats. They can swim as far as a half mile in open water, dive through water plumbing traps, and travel in sewer lines, even against strong water currents. Roof rats are agile climbers and can shinny the outside of three-inch-diameter pipes or any size pipe within three inches of a wall!

RATS HAVE LIVED WITH HUMANS FOR A LONG TIME. IN FACT, RAT AND MICE BONES HAVE BEEN FOUND IN CAVES WHERE CAVEMEN LIVED!

By the way, muriphobia and suriphobia are terms for the fear of mice!

ONE MORE NAUSEATING CROSSWORD!

FILL IN THE BLANKS AND SOLVE DISTASTEFUL PUZZLE #4:

ACROSS

3. Fill in the blank: Cod _____ Oil. (Hint: rhymes with "river")

5. This item eaten on *Fear Factor* was 100 years old; birds lay it.

7. On one episode of *Fear Factor*, players had to eat breakfast cereal made of this creature; it is a worm that spins silk thread.

10. During a Halloween *Fear Factor*, contestants had to eat this kind of beetle; it's a word that means "bad smell."

11. Theses tiny critters are similar to maggots, and players had to bob for chicken feet in a tub full of them. (Hint: rhymes with "tax terms") 2 words

12. Players stomped on worms to make this drink. (Hint: rhymes with "vine")

13. This type of earthworm is tasty to fish and birds, not so much to humans. (Hint: first word rhymes with "fright," and second word is how it gets around) 2 words

14. *Fear Factor* players had to drink the fermented guts of this sea creature. (Hint: rhymes with "kid")

DOWN

1. Players had to take off their shoes and walk over broken pieces of this; what windows are made of.

2. This kind of bull was ridden to determine how many bull parts were to be eaten; it's not a real bull.

4. This red, juicy fruit was eaten by contestants out of a box also filled with flies; it's a popular flavor of milkshake, as in "chocolate, vanilla, and _____."

6. Players had to eat a big egg that comes from this big bird; a false tale was that this bird would stick its head in the ground if it was frightened.

8. Contestants played slot machines to determine how many sheep, cow, and fish eyes they would have to eat when *Fear Factor* visited this gambling city. 2 words

9. The ham part of *Fear Factor* ham and eggs is made of this. (Hint: first word rhymes with "big," second word is what your doctor will ask you to stick out before you say "ahhh") 2 words

Answers on page 76

57

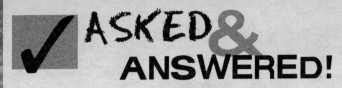

✔ ASKED & ANSWERED!

WE ASKED PLAYERS WHAT THEIR STRATEGY OR PERSONAL MOTIVATION WAS TO WIN ON *FEAR FACTOR*. HERE'S WHAT THEY SAID.

✔ "I am motivated to be on the show to put my years of experience gained being crazy to good use."

✔ "My boyfriend doesn't think I'm capable of eating a bug without convulsing."

✔ "I have no fears and will eat anything! In eighth grade, I ate two June bugs for thirteen dollars."

✔ "To prove that, in my thirties, I've developed my mind enough to eat any bug, etc., and conquer any physical stunt I put my mind to."

✔ "The eating bugs thing . . . I'm going to read up on third-world countries and their eating habits. Knowing I'm not the only one in the world eating the biggest, ugliest grasshopper . . . made will make me feel more confident about chowing down on it."

ON THE SUBJECT OF
FEAR

QUOTES FROM FAMOUS PEOPLE—PAST AND PRESENT

"Courage is resistance to fear, mastery of fear—not absence of fear."
—*Mark Twain*

"The greatest mistake you can make in life is to be continually fearing you will make one."
—*Elbert Hubbard*

"None but a coward dares to boast that he has never known fear."
—*Ferdinand Foch*

"You see what power is—holding someone else's fear in your hand and showing it to them!"
—*Amy Tan*

"Nothing in life is to be feared, it is only to be understood."
—*Marie Curie*

"Fear is that little darkroom where negatives are developed."
—*Michael Pritchard*

"Keep your fears to yourself, but share your courage with others."
—*Robert Louis Stevenson*

"Go forth to meet the shadowy future, without fear."
—*Henry Wadsworth Longfellow*

"Whatever you fear most has no power—it is your fear that has the power."
—*Oprah Winfrey*

"The only real prison is fear, and the only real freedom is freedom from fear."
—*Aung San Suu Kyi*

"Fear of a name increases fear of the thing itself."
—*J. K. Rowling*

"The only thing we have to fear is fear itself."
—*Franklin D. Roosevelt*

SOME INTERNATIONAL FOODS AREN'T TO EVERYONE'S TASTE!

SEE IF YOU CAN STOMACH THESE MEALS:

• Sannakji, from Korea, is a delicacy that fights back. Chefs will slice off a tentacle of a small live octopus and bring it to the table. The tentacle goes down squirming, which is considered the highlight of the experience—along with the slight vacuum action of its suction cups.

• Basashi is raw horse meat from Japan, often smothered in soy sauce but served other ways, too. In fact, there's a Basashi-flavored ice cream!

• Casu Marzu from Sardinia is maggot cheese. To make it, you start with pecorino, an ordinary Italian sheep-milk cheese. You leave it out in the sun, so flies can lay their eggs in it. The larvae become maggots, whose respiration causes the cheese to ferment into a particularly creamy concoction.

• Tripe, from England, is the stomach lining of a cow. It is white and translucent, rubbery in texture, and is served boiled with onions.

• Black pudding, from England, is also known as blood sausage. It's a pudding made of curdled and boiled pig's blood, mixed with chunks of pork fat (for texture and juiciness) and spices, then stuffed into a sausage casing.

• Czarnina, from Poland, is duck-blood soup.

- Seonjiguk is also from Korea. It's pig-blood curd soup.

- Dinuguan is pig-blood stew from the Philippines.

- Balut, also from the Philippines, is basically a boiled embryo of a duck, still in its egg. It's called "the treat with feet" on *Fear Factor*, because it has them. And a beak.

- Of course, we in the U.S. have some strange tastes, too. In fact, an American university entomology club went on television recently with their recipes for Banana Worm Bread, Rootworm Beetle Dip, Candied Crickets, Mealworm Fried Rice, Corn Borer Cornbread, and Chocolate-Covered Grasshoppers!

The PHobiC FaCt FiLe

BLENNOPHOBIA OR MYXOPHOBIA IS THE FEAR OF SLIME!

As one of the slimiest creatures, a single hagfish can produce over a gallon of slime. As a defense mechanism, hagfish use their thick slime to choke the gills of predatory fish. Hagfish escape from their own slime by tying themselves in knots and squeezing the slime from their bodies.

WATCH OUT! A TYPICAL SLIMY GARDEN SNAIL CAN MOVE UP TO 23 INCHES PER HOUR!

By the way, the fear of motion or movement is kinetophobia or kinesophobia.

STRAIGHT FROM A PLAYER'S MOUTH!

AN INTERVIEW WITH A COMPETITIVE COCKROACH COUPLE

FEAR FACTOR: What did you think when you first saw all those huge cockroaches?

JASON: The smell when we walked into the room was unbelievable. When Joe said "Go," I remember just throwing my face down in that nasty, stinky box. I just grabbed as many as I could, I just wanted to hurry up, because going first, the pressure was on and we had to set a high bar. I was amazed I could fit five of those roaches in my mouth. It was unreal because they were clawing, biting, pooping. It was disgusting.

FEAR FACTOR: Misti, were you amazed that you also could fit five roaches in your mouth?

MISTI: Jason and I had talked about just transferring one roach at a time. But once we started, it was, like, let's do whatever we have to do. I was just as surprised as anybody when I spit out that first mouthful of about four or five roaches. I had no idea that it would be four or five roaches in my mouth.

FEAR FACTOR: Did you two have a special strategy in place?

MISTI: Well, right before we began, I knew how I was going to have to position my feet to turn, to twist really fast back to the other box. And I think I had an advantage over the other team because I'm longer. Jason and I wanted it to be where, as soon as the roaches were in my mouth, I would immediately turn and he would immediately go down for more. So he was never having to wait with roaches in his mouth. There were a few times where they were biting my lips and getting a good hold in my mouth and I had to shake them off, and that was horrible.

FEAR FACTOR: You two were definitely in a zone. Jason, at one point you banged your head and had started bleeding a little, but you never seemed to let that affect your rhythm.

JASON: I couldn't tell that I was cut when I was going down. I went down so many times. I knew that I had so many roaches in my face at different times, I was knocking them away, so I couldn't tell if one of them just scratched me or whatever. But once I got through and I could feel up there, I felt a little knot, so I knew I must have banged something.

FEAR FACTOR: Did you give each other a pep talk to get through this?

JASON: When we were strategizing about how we were going to do it, I know we were both kind of in shock to think what we had to do as far as putting those things in our mouths and transferring them. But right then, I was like, "Look, this is not funny. We've got to get serious about this." I said, "I don't know how we're going to be able to do as far as the number, but as soon as you get them, you blow them out and be aggressive with them."

DID YOU KNOW... ?

- In one episode, an estimated 500,000 worms were dumped on each contestant. *What a horrible way to get dumped!*

- In the same episode, 500 pounds of fish were dumped on each contestant. *I hope they got some tartar sauce to go with that!*

- The camel spider, used in *Fear Factor* stunts, is native to the deserts of Iraq and can grow up to 10 inches in length. *Gee, their cobwebs must be huge (and a pain to sweep out of corners)!*

- In the shocking electric-maze stunt, the metal handcuffs used in the stunt acted as a conductor, ensuring that each time a contestant was shocked their partner would also feel it. *It's like they say, misery loves company!*

- Some of the pieces of cow stomach used in the stunt where players tossed them to each other weighed up to twenty pounds. *No wonder they could hardly stomach that stunt!*

- Moray eels, featured on *Fear Factor* a few times, are equipped with strong, razor-sharp teeth that enable them to seize and hold on to their prey or inflict serious injury on their enemies. *That's some trivia you can really sink your teeth into!*

- Moray eels have a double-hinged jaw, which enables them to eat large prey several times the size of their own heads. *As long as they keep their mouths shut when they chew!*

- In 2003, *Fear Factor* won the Teen Choice Award for "Grossest Reality TV Moment," which was eating squid guts. *An honor . . . or, a horror. You decide!*

WORD SEARCH 3:

HOW ABOUT ONE MORE GROSS WORD SEARCH?

FIND AND CIRCLE THE WORDS BELOW TO DISCOVER

THE SECRET MESSAGE:

PUZZLE WORDS

DOUGHNUTS	PICKLED
EARTHWORM	PIZZA
GRAVY	SHAME
GREASY	SOUR
GRINDER	TASTY
MILKSHAKE	WATER
OSTRICH	YUCK

Once you've uncovered all these gross words, circle the first 15 leftover letters to find a hidden message.

Answers on page 78

W	A	Y	T	C	H	W	H	A	T	M	S
Y	P	O	U	G	R	E	A	S	Y	I	T
U	I	E	E	C	Y	A	T	I	Y	L	U
M	Z	J	A	V	K	Z	O	J	H	K	N
R	Z	W	A	R	Y	S	Q	K	V	S	H
U	A	R	G	T	T	E	H	M	K	H	G
O	G	C	S	R	D	H	M	K	L	A	U
S	V	A	I	Q	I	P	W	A	M	K	O
Z	T	C	P	M	T	N	N	O	H	E	D
P	H	T	L	L	X	C	D	H	R	S	R
D	E	L	K	C	I	P	K	E	R	M	Y
N	N	T	Y	P	W	A	T	E	R	D	Y

TEST YOURSELF WITH THIS JUMBO *FEAR FACTOR*

TRIVIA QUIZ!

ANSWER THESE GROSS-STUNT QUESTIONS AND SEE HOW YOU RATE.

Q: What was the very first gross stunt on *Fear Factor*?

a. Licking bullfrogs
b. Swimming with crabs
c. Lying in a rat pit
d. Gargling with pig blood

Answer: c, A truly ratty experience!

Q: In what year did *Fear Factor* premiere?

a. 1999
b. 2000
c. 2001
d. 2002

Answer: c, 2001, a Gross Odyssey!

Q: During the Worm Coffin stunt, how many worms did vegetarian Amanda eat?

a. None
b. One
c. Two
d. Five

Answer: a, She quit instead of eating any!

Q: During the Beetle Bowl stunt, what did players have to do to determine how many beetles they had to eat?

a. Balance a bowl filled with beetles on their heads
b. Bowl at a bowling alley
c. Pick a piece of paper out of a bowl filled with beetles
d. None of the above

Answer: b. If they bowled a strike, they didn't have to eat any!

Q: In what setting did *Fear Factor* contestants compete in the Pig Feast stunt?

a. Amusement park
b. Pig farm
c. Dark basement
d. Chinese restaurant

Answer: d. Their fortune cookies told them what part they had to eat!

Q: How many players were able to complete the *Fear Factor* spaghetti stunt?

a. None
b. One
c. Two
d. Three

Answer: a. They all choked!

Q: In the *Fear Factor* Billiards stunt, the billiard balls had one of four symbols on them: an egg, an ant, a squid, and a what?

a. Cockroach
b. Snake
c. Chili pepper
d. Worm

Answer: c. Representing a hot, hot chili pepper!

Q: Which of the following was NOT an ingredient for the Blender of Fear stunt?

a. Pig brains
b. Cow eyes
c. Lamb spleen
d. Fish sauce

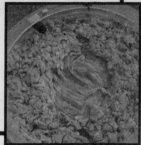

Answer: c, Because taking a little lamb's spleen would be too mean!

Q: In the Bobbing in Wax Worms stunt, what was buried in the deep plastic container, amongst 25,000 squirming maggot worms?

a. Chicken feet
b. Keys
c. Rings
d. Moldy cheese

Answer: a, And it was quite a feat to grab them!

Q: In the Eat Brains stunt, what card game did the contestants play to determine how much brains they had to eat?

a. Canasta
b. Go fish
c. War
d. Poker

Answer: d, And the players who ate those cow brains were royally flushed!

Q: Players had to nab what kind of fruit with their mouths out of a snake-filled tank in the Snake Face-Off stunt?

a. Pineapples
b. Plums
c. Pears
d. Peaches

Answer: b. And it was "plum" excitig, too!

Q: During the Torment Cell stunt, celebrity players had to share the small space with superworms, millipedes, and 20 of what kind of creature?

a. Emperor scorpions
b. Ladybugs
c. Tarantulas
d. Gecko lizards

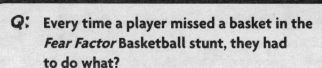

Answer: a. With a snip, snip here, and a sting, sting there!

Q: Every time a player missed a basket in the *Fear Factor* Basketball stunt, they had to do what?

a. Drink a glass of squid ink
b. Drink a glass of blended worms and cockroaches
c. Eat a buffalo tongue
d. Swim across a pool filled with alligators

Answer: b. And they couldn't *dribble* it, either!

Q: **In the Skunk Tunnel stunt, how many dead skunks did players have to collect in the pitch-black tunnel?**

a. Two

b. Five

c. Four

d. Three

Answer: d; The players were peppy, but the smell was le pew!

Q: **What liquid replaced milk in the Breakfast of Champions stunt?**

a. Sour squid ink

b. Cow eyeball juice

c. Bitter brine

d. Pig intestinal fluid

Answer: c; Aye, mateys! And the saltier, the better! Yar!

SO, HOW DID YOU DO?

COUNT THE NUMBER OF QUESTIONS YOU GOT RIGHT, AND SEE WHERE YOU RATE ON THE FEAR FACTOR EXPERT YUCK-O-METER!

0-3 Correct = Yuck-O-Meter Expert rating ★ You're a *Fear Factor* Newbie; you recently discovered the show, or else you hide your eyes during the gross parts!

4-6 Correct = Yuck-O-Meter Expert rating ★★ You're a *Fear Factor* Rookie; you are gross-knowledgeable, but you'd probably still scream if you got a bug on you!

7-9 Correct = Yuck-O-Meter Expert rating ★★★ You're a *Fear Factor* Semi-Pro; you'll play with bugs and spiders, but snakes and alligators give you the willies!

10-12 Correct = Yuck-O-Meter Expert rating ★★★★ You're a *Fear Factor* Pro; you could probably be convinced to eat a cockroach yourself!

13-15 Correct = Yuck-O-Meter Expert rating ★★★★★ You're a *Fear Factor* All-Star; your friends should never, ever invite you over for Sunday dinner with their family. More importantly . . . **FEAR IS NOT A FACTOR FOR YOU!**

ANSWERS

Crossword #1 from page 7:

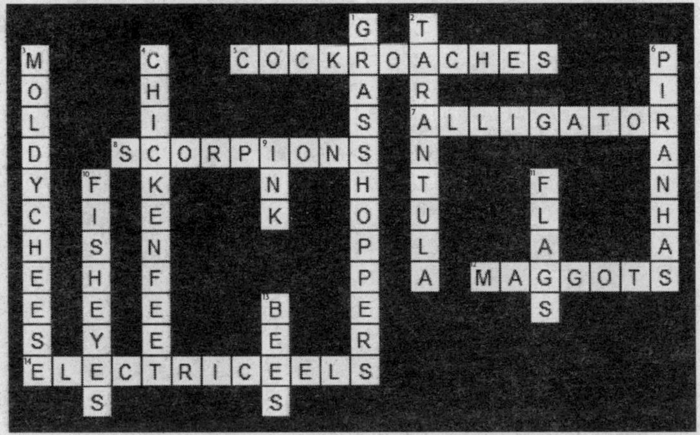

1 GRASSHOPPERS
2 TARANTULA
3 MOLDYCHEESES
4 CHICKENFEET
5 COCKROACHES
6 PIRANHAS
7 ALLIGATOR
8 SCORPIONS
9 INK
10 FISHEYES
11 FLAGS
12 MAGGOTS
13 BEES
14 ELECTRICEELS

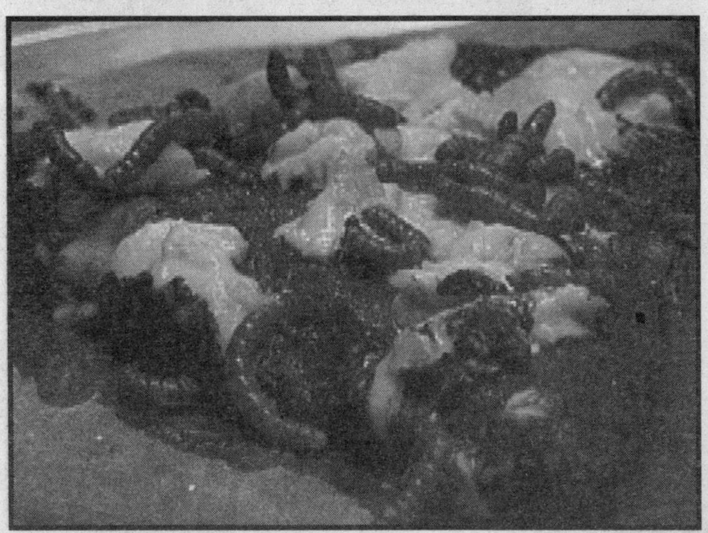

ANSWERS

Crossword #2 from page 17:

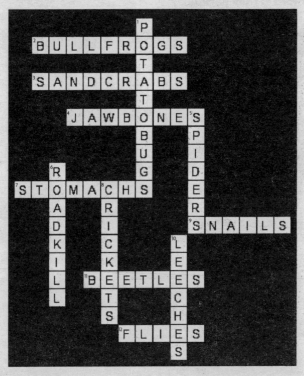

Across:
- BULLFROGS
- SANDCRABS
- JAWBONES
- STOMACHS
- SNAILS
- BEETLES
- FLIES

Down:
- POTATBUG
- SPIDER
- ROADKILL
- CRICKETS
- LEECHES

ANSWERS

Crossword #3 from page 35:

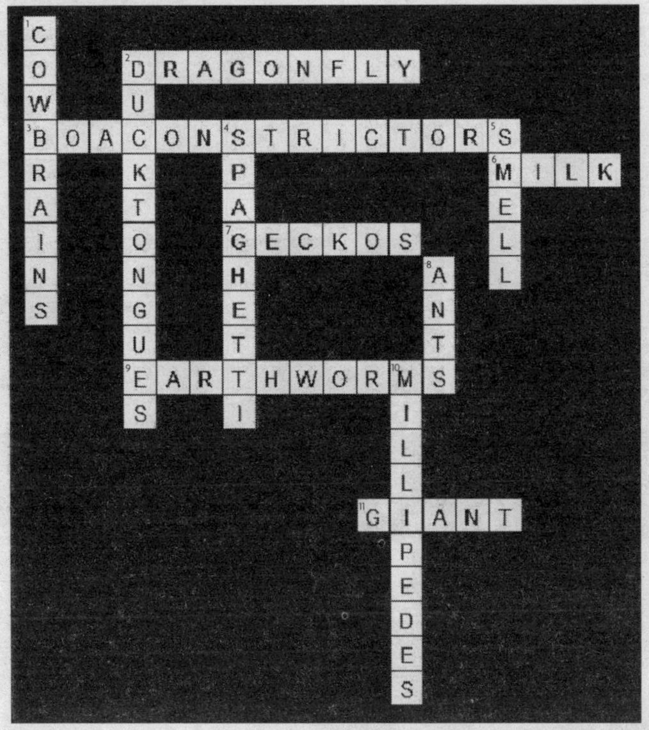

1 COWBRAINS
2 DRAGONFLY
2 DUCKTONGUES
3 BOACONSTRICTORS
4 SPAGHETTI
5 SMELL
6 MILK
7 GECKOS
8 ANTS
9 EARTHWORMS
10 MILLIPEDES
11 GIANT

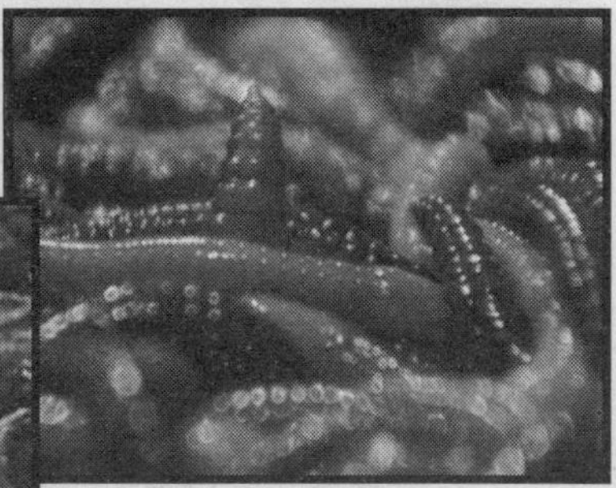

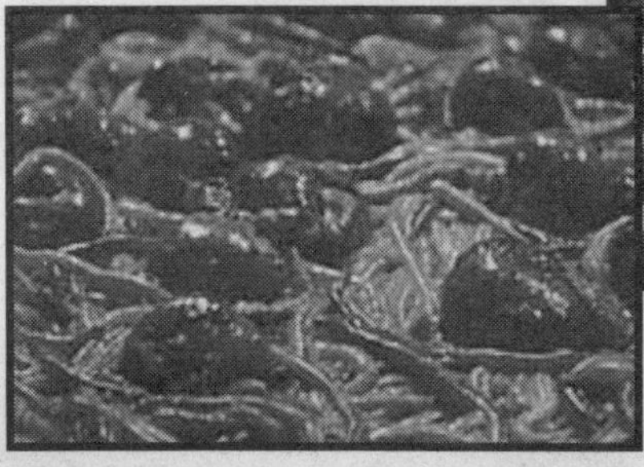

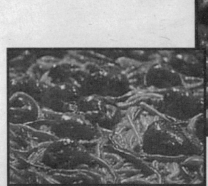

ANSWERS

Crossword #4 from page 57:

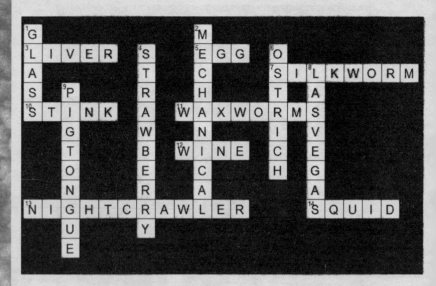

ANSWERS

ANSWERS FOR WORD SEARCH 1 from page 25:

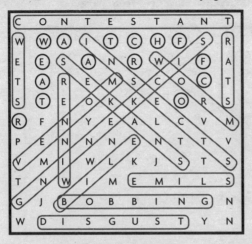

Secret Message: WATCH *FEAR FACTOR*

ANSWERS FOR WORD SEARCH 2 from page 47:

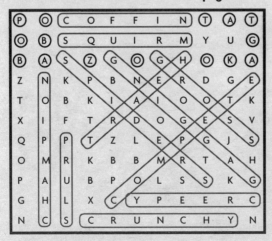

Secret Message: POTATO BUG BAZOOKA

ANSWERS

ANSWERS FOR WORD SEARCH 3 from page 67:

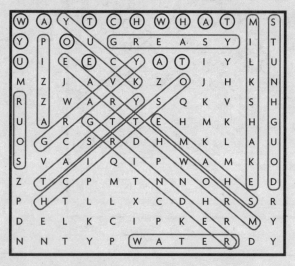

Secret Message: WATCH WHAT YOU EAT